THE FLOW OF LIFE

"GOD WILL LEAD YOU BESIDE THE STILL WATERS"

~Poems and Inspirations~

TENESHIA TATE

Glimpse of Glory Christian Book Publishing
P O Box 94131
Birmingham, Al 35220

Unless otherwise noted Scriptures are taken from King James Version Bible.

ISBN: 978-0-9833221-4-6

Printed in the United States of America

CONTENTS

THE FLOW OF LIFE

ACKNOWLEDGEMENTS

~

If it weren't for my Heavenly Father, I would not be here or where I am today, so I must first start by praising and giving Him thanks. You are such an amazing friend, comforter, provider and healer. You are the One that will always be here with me through whatever situation I face in life. Thank you, God! I thank You for all that You have done for me, what You are doing in my life right now, and for what You are about to do. Without You I am nothing.

To my husband Bobby Tate, I love you. Thanks for showing me the true meaning of stepping out; not just in your words, but in your actions, too. I draw strength from you. You have shared many times that if I don't try, I will never know. You taught me that if I want something in life, it is okay to step out on Faith. You are one of my greatest inspirations, and I thank God for placing you in my life. Bobby, I love you and thank you for all of the life lessons that you have taught me, and for pushing, encouraging, and standing by me on my journey.

I thank God for my daughter, Ron'Nesha. You are my world, and my absolute balance. There have been many times when I felt like giving up, and did not know which way to turn, but you spoke life into me. I know without a shadow of a doubt, if it were not for you, I would have given up. On several occasions, it almost felt like you were the adult and I was the child. I am forever grateful that God blessed me with such caring, loving and encouraging daughter. I love you, Ron'Nesha.

Thanks to my mother, Doris Marshall, for carrying me nine months and giving birth to such talented, anointed, and blessed child who has grown into the virtuous woman that God has called me to be. Thank you so much for pushing me to use my gifts and talents. I look at you and smile because you are the sweetest mother a girl could ask for. No one could ever take your place.

To my mother-in-law, Debra Tate, thank you for loving me like the daughter you never had. I do not know of a mother and daughter-in-law that have such a special bond as ours. I can remember when I first met you. You told me you dreamt that God was going to give you a spiritual daughter-in-law, and then came me. I know that we do not see eye to eye on everything, but you are my best friend. You always uplift me and encourage me in ways you could never imagine, and it's genuine too. I love you until no end.

I am sending a special thanks to my sister, my motivator, my inspiration, my encourager, Author and Evangelist Yolanda Marshall-Nickerson. Thank you for inspiring me, pushing me, talking to me, and encouraging me through my process. You have always had faith in me, and you spoke life into me when I felt like throwing in the towel. You saw the things God had in store for me long before I ever saw them. You have helped me to see that I can do anything I put my mind to. I look up to you, and I love you for always being there to coach me through certain situations.

To my friends, Joannie and Jokeitha, I thank the Lord for placing each of you in my life. Words could never express how blessed I am to have both of you in my corner. Thank you all for always being there to listen when I need someone to talk to, and for being my strength and inspiration as well. You both have helped me on my journey in so many ways, and I appreciate both of you.

To my siblings, I would not trade any of you for the world. No matter what struggles, trials or tribulations we endured growing up, we all overcame them, and we are all still here. Praise God! Zacchaeus, Kezia, Krashawna, Eric, Berniece, La'Tonya, Yolanda, Kevin, Ronald, Devona, Cathy, and Frederick, thank each of you for supporting, encouraging and praying for me. You all have played a major role in my life. You all have sown into my life in so many ways; each of you has made me feel so very special. I love you all.

To my brother-in-laws Charles, Terrence, Elijah, Darius, Frank, Rolondus, Ladarrius, Larry, and to my only sister-in-law, Cheryl, I love each of you. When God placed you all in my life, He knew what He was doing. I am so grateful to have each of you in my life, and I appreciate you all for loving and embracing me, too.

To my many nieces, nephews, great nieces and great nephews, I love each of you, and I would like for you all to know that there is nothing too hard for God. You can be and do anything you set out to do. Never give up on your dreams, and never let anyone tell you that you cannot do something because you can.

To all my friends, loved ones, and supporters, I would like to thank you all for being a blessing in my life. I gain strength from knowing that I have people who I can count on and call on in the time of need. My journey has not been easy, but it has been worth it.

PREFACE

~

When I was growing up, I knew exactly what God called me to be. No one had to tell me because my gift spoke for itself. Many people go through life wondering, pondering, and trying to figure out what their gift may be, but God showed me early in life. My gift was right in front of me, and I know that if you look closely, you will see what your gift is, too. I would like to share the two gifts that I now fully embrace.

The first gift that I have is singing. I remember when growing up, I used to get up in the mornings and sing in front of the bathroom or bedroom mirror. My brother Zack would always say, "Nesha, you are always singing." I can also remember singing while sitting in the back seat of my father's car when we were traveling to various places, and he would say, "I hear you, baby." My mother tells me often that I need to use my gift or God will take it and give it to someone who will appreciate it. It is now 2015, and I am 34 years old, finally deciding to pursue and use my gifts and talents. I love music so much, and I am thankful that God blessed me with the voice to be a blessing to people.

The second gift that I have is exhortation ("gift of encouragement"). I discovered this gift as a teenager. I would always find myself inspiring, motivating and encouraging others. It did not matter if it was through just talking, or writing a poem. I could see, sense and feel the hurt and pain that people were dealing with, so I began to speak life into them. It went from encouraging and motivating sometimes to encouraging and motivating on a daily basis. I still do the same thing now. We never know what people are going through or what they need, so I choose to be the one to be a positive force in their lives by encouraging them. People often say after I encourage them, "Thank you, Teneshia. I needed that. It was right on time."

God has given me the gift to sing and write, not only to encourage you, but to encourage myself as well. I plan to use these two gifts daily to help those of you who are in need. You may now find yourself in need of deliverance, peace, joy, happiness, and much more, and I believe that you will experience those things as you read this book. I decided to write this book because I have no doubt in my mind that it will be a blessing to you and so many others.

This book will help you and serve as a reminder that better days are ahead of you after your storm is over. After you go through the trials, tribulations and hard times, you can still rise above it all. I want you to know that no matter what has happened, what may be happening in your life right now, or what may become of your life, you have the power to move mountains. Whatever it is that you want or need, you can have it by asking your Heavenly Father, believing and positioning yourself to receive it.

I encourage you to embrace all the blessing that God is going to pour into your life. He is ready to bless each of you exceedingly and abundantly.

~

POEMS

~

Allow these poems to speak to your heart and lift your spirit.

1

CHANGES

~

Life changes take a lot out of you

Some drain, stress, and make you feel blue

Causing tears to flow, and your mood to change

One thing for sure, the pain makes you feel strange

Making you want to throw in the towel

Having you angry with each passing hour

We always wonder why we're up one day, and the next we're down

Not realizing it's the changes that make you frown

The anger, the sadness and the bitterness too

The tears, loneliness, all the things that upsets you

I love the changes that life will bring

The ones that feels like a warm day in the spring

The laughter and peace that warms your heart

Just a few leading to a great start

The changes, good, bad and trying ones too

They are all the things that help with the growth of you

What will you make of your change?

2

DESIRE

~

Waking up in the mornings, we have a fresh start

To be happy, kind, and to love from our heart

Will we be caring, mean, or choose to be sweet

Faithful, honest, or decide to cheat

Will we steal, kill, or will we destroy

Start a family, have a girl or a boy

Change, move forward, or will we stay the same

Take initiative, be accountable, or point the finger and blame

Your desires are your thoughts, whether bad or good

If you choose the wrong choices in life, the consequences should be understood

My desire is in no way to take the wrong path, never ever in life

I plan to always walk straight, and let God fight the fight

Desires starts as just a thought hiding in your head

It's a book, your book that has to be fed

So choose wisely, think deeply on which way you will go

For once that desire is fed your desire will begin to grow

3

TRY

~

Now that I understand, I can clearly see

The choices I make are all up to me

A doctor, a lawyer, an astronaut in the sky

A Fortune 500 business, you never know until you try

If your dream is to be a rock star, dancer, actress too

Start rehearsing how to make all those wishes come true

What others say or think does not mean you stop

With God all is possible and He won't let you drop

Times may get hard and you think, "Lord, why, why?"

But guess what? Success is in arms reach, so go ahead and try

Be the BEST at whatever you do

Be a humble servant in the name of God, and He will guide you through

Striving to be the best can be very hard

But all things are possible when you proceed with God!

4

DETERMINATION

~

Success is measured by your faith and your determination

Go for it and go after it with no hesitation

You will encounter many detours along your journey

But press through the rain, through the pain, even when it's stormy

God has the perfect plan for you that only you can fulfill

Don't give up, and don't give in, you just stand still

Watch God show up mighty on your behalf

He'll break the chains, give you the tools you need, and even make you laugh

Stay focused, remain positive, and continue with your preparation

To reach your goal, fulfill your dream, and providing motivation

Keep the faith, yield to God, and continue on your route

Because only the determined, including the faithful will be able to shout

Dance, praise, and reap the harvest

Of what you've sowed, what you've watered, and what you've started

5

SHOUT NOW

~

As I sat alone, quietly in my car

I began to praise God for bringing me this far

As I look back over my life, and how far I've come

I think about the mess that God has delivered me from

I could hear his voice saying, "Rejoice and shout now"

I could have called you home, when your house got all shot up

But I spared your life to minister in this world that's so corrupt

I could have been invalid, when you had your stroke

But your place is here on earth to mend the spiritually broke

I definitely could have sucked out your breath, when you tried suicide

But I said, "NOO! I need that child on my side

Be thankful for your voice, your vision, and your hands,

Your calling is to help my people, and that is my demand

Shout Now! Shout Now! My anointed one!

What I have in store for you, is pay for all the work you've done

Your territory has increased; that will continue

And anytime you go astray, before that I forgive you

Shout Now! Shout Now! And worship me

And anointing will continue to transfer from Me to thee!

6

DON'T GO BACK

~

I delivered you from the enemy on numerous occasions

But you go back, turn against me, and reopen the abrasions

Having to face the same battles I've already fought for you

Healing your pain, wiping your tears, and pulling you through

Why put yourself in the same exact situation

Of being hurt, confused, and feeling agitation

When I deliver you from the hands of the enemy

I expect you to go, grow and spread the Word to many

Of how I brought you out, and fought the fight for you

I spoke for you, protected you, and left nothing for you to do

Don't go back, don't look back, and don't you be afraid

Just look up, keep moving forward, and don't you be dismayed

I've given you the power, and the tools to stand with your head held high

While pressing your way, and not going back, but to keep walking right on by

7

REJOICE

~

I done made a mess

Of so many things in my life

I have only me to blame

For all the hardships, slips and strife

My weeping has endured

Both days and countless nights

Then God appeared

And all I could see was His shining light

I told him I was giving up

And that I was throwing in the towel

He chuckled when I said that

Then said, "No my beautiful flower"

I became strong and tall like an oak tree

With branches spreading here and there

Sprouting and becoming the woman He wanted me to be

Now I'm that tree that will not bend

No matter how hard the wind blows

He taught, showed and guided me

To the knowledge I needed to know

Since then I've been rejoicing

Any and everywhere I go

I rejoice, rejoice, and rejoice

And nobody else needs to know

All I wanted was God to bring me peace

Peace in knowing, peace in need

Peace in whatever I desired; everything I need

I urge you to Rejoice Now

Because your blessing is near

Rejoice now because when God delivers,

You'll be ready, no doubt, and no questions, just clear.

8

SEARCH NO MORE

~

I exhausted myself searching for meaning

Going up one way, coming down the other

That didn't work, so I started to spin

Out of control, getting sick on the merry go round

I met a spirit man one day, who told me, "Plant your feet flat on the ground."

Immediately my world began to change

He pointed out why all my endeavors ended up the same

He told me I could get to where I needed to be

That I had to humble myself, let my spirit be

All I needed to do was go to him (Our Father)

Because every time I tried by myself, I fell harder

God told me, "Search No More", I am all you need

Bend on your knees, give me your heart, and I'll plant the seed

Fast, pray, and meditate on my word

Listen to me, follow me, and obey everything you heard

Peace of mind and love can't be bought

In the spirit world, life is different that's what we are taught

Come on to me, and submit your all

If you don't, you'll keep hitting that wall

What you're searching for is right here in me

So come this way, I will teach you, and you'll be free

9

OVERCOMER

~

No matter what the circumstance, situation or condition may be

You should always uplift and encourage each other, and try to agree

Agree on coming to a common ground

Agree on not letting your issues keep you bound

I've been there, done that, and endured so much pain

And now I'm to the point, I stay away from the rain

The tears, the sickness, my sadness that came

Are slowly, but surely leaving, even the pain

I can feel myself getting up from the ground

Singing, praising, and prancing around

The bitter and anger that tried to overtake me

Has made me stronger, wiser, and has set me free

I'm an overcomer, an overcomer can't you see

That God has changed me, transformed me, and has showed me exactly how to be

You can be an overcomer too

Just give your life to God, trust Him, and let Him guide you through.

10

AIM HIGH

~

Aim High! Can seem like a hard thing to do

But really how high you get is all inside of you

You can have it, name it, and anything you want to be

I have a mantra I say all day, "Success is up to me."

I'm a poet already; maybe I'll try my hand at song-writing

I hype myself up, speak life into the air, and hum in quiet hiding

I strive to be the best, for me, there's no other way

For I am an anointed child of God, and that ain't no cliché'

Listen, I used to be afraid to reach, for fearing I would fail

But that's nothing but mere bondage, and I ain't fond of jail

If you Aim and Aim High, and no matter what don't give in

When it's all said and done, it's clear that you will win!

11

THE STRUGGLES

~

While I drive down a long, dark, winding road

I can't help but think of traumas that had my life on hold

Events that really tore at me, while clouds followed me all day

The things I promised I would never tell anyone, even to this day

The struggles of dealing with low self-esteem

When I was young I was molested, and that changed everything

The struggles of going through life not having a lot of money

Wanting things and wanting to do things, being told, "Sorry honey!"

The struggles as a child of bullying and being called names

I realized they were young, silly, and playing games

I wanted to be a friend and encourage them on their path

No, but they looked at me like I was tore down and smelling like I needed a bath

You see, everyone knows where they've been, but not where they're going

Always treat others with respect and love

Treat people how you like to be treated

Because Karma comes back, knocks you down, and there you'll be

12

TOTALLY FREE

~

"Let Go and Let God"

That's what the spirits tell me

"He's your comforter, light, shelter and rod"

My ancestors told me not to worry

About anything or how it unfolds

But I refuse to be bound and confused

Wondering what the outcome will be

All I had to do is listen to God

And I would be Totally Free

The disobedience, I'm guilty, speaking about me

I took in all the criticism and lies

That people would do and say to me

I'd walk around hurting, head down and eyes glazed

So much I couldn't see

All I had to do was go to my secret corner, spend time with God

And I would be Totally Free

I used to get unraveled, snippy, and really mean

Until God showed me deliverance, love, joy and wisdom to accept

What I cannot change

And I broke the chains of bondage

And I am Totally Free

13

PHILIPPIANS 4:13

~

"I can do all things through Christ which strengthens me"

God is saying, "I can change you and help you to be"

The best woman, man, boy or girl

Help you to see the light and change your whole world

Many times you may feel the load is too heavy

Well that's simply because you try to take on the load, that I should carry

I've already fought all your battles for you

Endured the pain, died on the cross and I rose for you

So that you may have life, and have it more abundantly

To enjoy the riches of the world, live happily, and be free

My child you need to know by reading Philippians 4:13

There's nothing that a man, job or even the world can bring

That should make you fall down to the point of no return

I want you to get back up, laugh and have fun

Enjoy this life that I have given to you

Don't worry about the foolishness of the world, but unto Me stay true

For I've given you the strength no man can take

Whether it's a so called friend, family member or a fake

Know that you can do anything you desire because I've given you the strength and power

To get back up, stand tall, hold your head up and blossom like a flower

A beautiful flower, I say a beautiful flower can't you see

That you can do all things through me because I am the one that strengthens thee

14

THEY DON'T BELONG

~

At times we try to make things and people fit in

But it always seems like the more we try, we never win

Have you ever thought about it hard and long?

That that person or thing they just don't belong

They don't belong on the same path as you

When your blessings begin to flow you only need those who are true

True to you and true to the things that concerns you

No matter the circumstance, condition or what you go through

They'll be your motivation, and even a shoulder to lean on

And they will be there when everyone else is gone

Everything and everyone they just don't belong

They are your downfall, and stronghold, and just absolutely wrong

No matter how hard you try, cry or pray

They will never belong, not until the day

When God changes them, and make them new

They'll never belong on the same path as you.

They don't belong!

15

I WONDER WHY

~

When life isn't going the way I wish it would

I rack my brain wondering why? And never understood

How certain things would end up the way they do

But I can't run away from the question to myself, "Is it you?"

Is it me that can change the situation?

Is it me who cloaks myself in limitations?

I turn my anger inward, and to others I am mean

Then I have to remind myself that cruelty isn't clean

I wonder why when I do my best; I'm not rewarded like the rest

I'm scared to go the depth that is deeper

For it may show me the secrets I've been keeping

I wonder why children of God are mistreated

And mope around like I did feeling defeated

The tide will change, roles will be reversed

And those who are the last on Earth, in Heaven will be the first

I wonder why?

But I finally realized, it's not my place to justify

16

GOD IS NOT DONE WITH ME YET

~

When I wake up in the mornings, I plan to have a great day

I get dressed, look myself in the mirror and go about my way

I get in my car, and turn my music on

And I begin to listen to my favorite song

"Your Next in Line for a Miracle" yeah that's it

Because I know God is speaking to me and preparing me with

The proper attitude and mindset to start my day

And He's reminding me daily to always pray

I'm a work in progress, with a long way to go

I'll be patient as I blossom, and I'll take the journey slow

So take pride and know that He's working on you, too

Because He promised to be there, and to take us through

17

LIVE, LAUGH, LOVE

~

You should always "live, laugh, and love"

Wake up daily, and be ready to fly high like a dove

Many people are living in bondage every day

But I come to let you know, God loves you in a special way

He wants you to enjoy your life like never before

What He's done for you thus far is not it, there's more

So live, laugh, and always love

For God is sitting up high, watching over you from above

When He sees that you are living life and being sweet

He's going to bless you exceedingly all the way from head to feet

I was one that didn't know how to live, laugh, and love

Until one day, God revealed himself, and showed me His love

Now I live, laugh, and love even more

For I know when storms arise, God is there to bring them to shore

18

LOOKING OUT THE WINDOW

~

Looking out the window, I can clearly see

All of the wonderful blessings God have promised me

He reminds me that He has given me the power to do His will

Have and do anything in life my heart says fulfill

As I watch the people walk, jog, and run by

I begin to think about my life, and how I

Can be an inspiration to the world

Yes me, this country girl

Looking out the window, I see so many things

The sun, the trees, the flowers in the spring

My reflection in the window eases inner pain

I see myself running and jumping, releasing the chains

I envision myself, flying high up above

Soaring like an Eagle, or floating like a Dove

If you look out the window, you'll see

All the great and majestic blessings God have made for thee

19

DESTINY

~

Your destiny is the place that God has set aside for you

And contrary to what you might have planned

There's nothing you can do

You can go to school and get a degree then start a business

Just know God has plans for you

And you will be his witness

I've written down my plans

And I know what I want to do

All I must do is pray to God

And let Him guide me through

For in the end, if it's not in line with God's will

He'll redirect me to my destiny

So that prophecy will be fulfilled

That pondering and wondering about what to do is just a waste of time

Seek God, listen, let Him lead and things will be divine!

20

RESTORATION

~

You say your spirit's broken

You've been lied to and mistreated

God knows where your spirit is

And what He needs to feed it

Some person or situation

Has left you baffled and dismayed

Left your mind in tatters

Even though you always obey

Take a breath and be reassured

That getting up and standing tall

Is all that really matters

You will rise from that grave

But your faith must be intact

And you've got to do whatever necessary

To claim your spirit back

You and your faith in God

Will be your soul's salvation

And take the shining rod of hope

With the shield, you'll block the mob

Jesus will be there, He proclaimed just what to do

And that's when you emerge as whole, to see the restoration through

21

I WRITE

~

When the night is young, the stars peek through

And the moon begins to shine

I write a prayer that the sun's bright rays

Would nourish all the earth's lifelines

I write when I'm joyous, bouncing around and glad

I write when I'm frustrated, hostile and fighting mad

I'll write about the evils, going rampant in God's world

Makes me look at my daughter, she's my baby girl

When God gives you a vision, like the one He gave to me

I'll write to connect and touch you, and that comes back to me

22

HE KNOWS

~

It don't matter what you plan or what you do

God knows all, and He's looking right at you

He knows the time and place your life will end

So be mindful of your living and the message that you send

Folks are watching and looking up to you, in case you didn't know

Drop the negative, be positive and help someone to grow

He knows precisely what you do as the clock ticks day by day

It's best to take the humble route and always, always pray

He always know your thoughts and where you want to go

He's watching so be mindful of the seeds you choose to sow

He knows when the chips are down, and He feels when you are sad

He's aware of your infirmary, and he knows if it's bad

He knows when you're in the thick of things, and needing to be found

He'll catch you in the palm of his hands

So you don't fall on the muddy ground

It doesn't matter what you're faced with, if you panic and don't know what to do

Remember God knows everything, and his eyes are right on you

23

HOW MANY TIMES

~

How many times have you awaken unhappy and mad?

Fussing and carrying on about the thing you never had

Every rumble, tumble and tussle was for a reason

The elders will tell you, "Child it was only for a season."

How many times have you helped someone then they don't have your back

Give it to God and don't worry about it because it was a kind act

God sees and He smiles when you reach out to bless someone

In return He will bless you for all that you have done

How many times have you called on Jesus name?

Is it every day, hour, minute? It's all the same.

Keep in mind that if you are ashamed of him now

He will be ashamed of you in front of the Father

Then watch your life go into a fast spin, and things will get harder

How many times have you given up, in or given out

Being hard headed and not let God teach you what life's all about

The challenge is to stand still, look up, with your head held high

And watch how God protect you while the troubles pass you by

24

THE QUIET PLACE

~

Everyone should have their own secret quiet place

Where they can pray, cry and fall on their face

The quiet place where you can go and seek God

And finding this place should not be hard

If you need a renewal of the mind and some sense of peace

The quiet place is the perfect place where you can release

Release your mind from anything that's pressuring and bothering you

Where you can seek God, meditate or do what you want to do

Your quiet place is your place where you can bring

Lay, release, and carry everything to the king

This place is for only you and God to be alone

Where you can stay and listen to Him, until your issue is gone

It's a place where you can shout, laugh and sing

About all the blessings, favor and happiness that our Mighty

God will bring

If you don't have your own secret, quiet place set aside on today

I challenge you to find one, so you can go and spend some of your day

Do you have your own quiet place?

25

TAKE IT BACK

~

The sun does shine, and the sky is clear

And everything you've lost in all those years

The peace, the calm, your state of mind

You feel you've lost or left behind

TAKE IT BACK!

Your home foreclosed, your car repossessed

Your credit damaged, now you're depressed

That family member that's off Christ's path

Strung out on drugs, folks point and laugh

TAKE THEM BACK!

When you pray for them and love them

You're claiming the devil's defeat

And when you rebuke that slithery snake

It has no choice but to flee

TAKE THEM BACK!

If your faith, your trust, or your passion has faded

Say God Almighty! Ask him to lay his hands on and upgrade it

Snatch back the people or things that demons has stolen

Take it home, show it to God, and watch it go from stone to Golden!

26

DO YOUR PART

~

For many years, I've been writing and praying for God to bless me

To be the best poet, become successful, so that others can be free

But God replied, "I've done my part, now it's time you do your part"

So that's when I sat down at my table and I began to write

Thinking, and writing, and writing some more

Now I've begin to see things even clearer than before

Do your part my anointed child, wait, watch and see

How the doors of Heaven will begin to open, by Me and only Me

I've given you a roadmap, and the tools you need to use

But for so long you chose to delay, be lazy and refuse

To step out on faith and sow your seed

Writing your story, so that others can read

Now that you have caught on, and made the choice to do My will

Until your cup runs over, I will fill

I'm sharing my story with you reader, so you can do your part

Don't sit on your dreams; you have to make a start

When you start to walk in your destiny, and sow your seed

God will walk by your side, and make sure you succeed

You can't expect God to do His part, and do yours too

After you consult with Him and get your answer, then it'll be left up to you

So on today, I challenge you to get up, and start doing your part

One… two… three… Get ready, set, start

27

SIN FEELS GOOD

~

When I lived in the midst and haze of my sins

It felt so good, from the outside and within

I was buck wild, fornicating, with a man and not married

I thank God because through it all, it was me He still carried

My best friends were selfishness, envy, lust and greed

Those were the things I loved so much, and would always feed

My sins felt good, definitely, even being not right

The enemy had his claws in me from sun-up to night

When I used to steal as a young girl, just to fit in

No one could say a word to me, if it went against my sin

My sin felt good, and it had me very blind

To see that I was destroying myself, and in a bind

I used to be one of the meanest people you could ever meet

I found God, did a 180 turn, and landed on my feet

God told me that while sin felt good,

That I was lost way out in the woods

He showed me how I was destroying myself, and I was more in a bind

Because sin wasn't just in the body, it was eating at the mind

So take heed Christians, don't give the enemy a second more of your time

God's love washes away sin, I know he did mine.

28

UNCHANGEABLE

~

Your friends will change, and your job too

It don't matter, don't worry, God don't change, He'll be true

Your relationships will change, and people will walk away

I'm glad I worship the same God every single day

Just as He's enlarged territories long before time

He'll do the same for you and me at the drop of a dime

You say you need deliverance, and a brand new start

God hasn't changed his glorious ways, so you know he'll do his part

He's unchangeable, constant, eternal, and can make a blind man see

He has a blessing for everyone, including you and me

He's the Almighty you can count on, who will forever have your back

Whenever you begin to lose your way, He'll steer you back on track

And that's a fact!

29

IT IS EASY TO JUDGE

~

It is so easy to judge someone, to cover up your mess

Instead of blessing and encouraging them, to help them pass their test

Many people don't know the right way, so God put them on your path

So that you can bless and motivate them, and not talk down and laugh

Some people may be on their very last leg, and have nowhere to go

Instead of judging them and looking down on others, it's better to help them grow?

It's really easy to judge people, to try and hide your flaws

Instead of working and praying together to mend their battered walls

I used to be the one that judged, and I would always point the finger

But that all changed when I blocked my blessings, of becoming a poet and singer

God is the one, the only one that has the authority to judge

For Matthew 7:1 says, "Judge not, lests you be judged".

If this is not enough to help, in changing your evil ways

Just don't expect your road to be easy, and remember judgment day

30

I DECREE

~

When you decree something, it means it shall be so

It can be a situation needs to change, or someone has to go

I decree that your tomorrow will be better than your today

And that God bless you, in each and every way

I decree your health and strength is good, if not, will be restored

I decree your life is filled with goodwill that has you overjoyed

I decree that your finances overflow, and you are truly blessed

I decree you will stop worrying, and throw away the stress

I decree that you revel in a clear, renewed mind

I decree the things that bother you from now on, you leave behind

Jesus has opened windows of love, gain and overflow

"Go tell it on the mountain"

I decree that God is so!

31

BONDAGE

~

What can I say about Bondage? Nothing good, that's for sure

It can have your mind in shackles, your moods chaotic, and your pockets poor

Too many of us have lived in bondage for so many years

It has claimed our lives, caused division, and I won't mention the tears

The self loathing and past molestation kept me down for so long

Yet God raised my head, kissed my tears, and showed me I was wrong

So if you are holding on to past hurt and pains

Let go and let God or nothing will ever change

Forgive those who defiled you, and those who made you mad

Embrace your blessings, and tomorrows, and let go of being sad

You must want to be delivered, set free from being bound

Clean out the closet, sweep the back steps, and embrace a mind that's sound

Listen to God, follow Him and release that bondage!

~

INSPIRATIONS

~

Allow these inspirations to bless you like streams of water.

32

SPEAK LIFE AND STAND STILL

~

You may be faced with difficulty in your life today. You do not know what to do or which way to turn. I need for you to know that God has given you the power to overcome and conquer it. Speak life into your circumstance or condition, and watch it whiter away.

God is always there to see you through those difficult times that arise in your life. Storms will rage, but you must "Stand still". Don't be moved. Stare your storm(s) in the face, and tell it to "Be Still". There is "life in your tongue" and power in your words.

I will admit that at one point I could not stand still if you offered me the world. Life had to take me through the ringer more than once, and just when I thought I was about to lose my mind, a voice whispered to me, "Stand Still". At that point, I took heed. I am now whispering the same thing to you, "Stand Still".

33

LAUGH AND SMILE

~

I was one that was broken all the way down. I did not feel like smiling and pressing my way through my trials and tribulations. The road that I was traveling seemed dark and lonely. I encourage you to look in the mirror and say to yourself, "Nothing or no one can steal my joy because this joy that I have, the world didn't give it to me..."

God is with you every step of the way. I never understood it when people would say, "You are in control of your happiness," but now I do. If God woke you this morning with your health, strength, and you are in your right mind, then you have absolutely every reason to be happy. If you have a bad day, it is because you choose to. Make that choice to laugh and smile, and see how much better you are going to feel.

34

CLAIM IT

~

Set your mind on your goals, claim it, pray on it, and stand on your faith. Do not waver in your faith when you claim it. Just say it and get ready to receive it. And then sit back and watch the hand of God move and bring whatever it is to fruition that you have prayed to Him about.

35

IT IS OKAY TO CRY

~

If you are hurting on today, go to your secret, quiet place and cry like never before. It will make you feel a whole lot better. And just know that whatever it is that may be hindering you, trying to hold you back, and plaguing your spirit, has to release you.

The Bible tells us that "Weeping endureth for a night, but joy comes in the morning." Aren't you glad to know that you will "reap joy for the tears you sow"? When you cry, your tears are a symbol of cleansing your soul. God is changing some things in your life. Your joy is coming back. Your peace is coming back. Your strength is coming back. Just know that there is a shout behind every tear. So, shout now!

36

ENCOURAGE SOMEONE

~

You are here for a purpose. God woke you this morning because He has work for you to do. Ask Him how you can be a blessing to someone, even if it is just speaking a kind word to them.

Lift that person up and let them know that they are important. They just may need to know that they are loved and appreciated. They need you. It is so easy to be a negative influence, and we have plenty of it in the world today, so choose to be positive. God smiles on this and it makes Him happy.

37

CHANGE STARTS WITH YOU

~

No matter what happens on today, think before you act. Make sure the choice that you make will have a positive impact on you and someone else. Remember you are the change. Think before you speak! Think before you act! Think before you judge! Think before you say yes or no! When you think first, it helps you to make the best decisions possible.

38

YOU REAP WHAT YOU SOW

~

What you give is what you will reap. I do not know about you, but I love good things, positive returns, and favors. Plant good seeds on today and watch the harvest come back to you. Make the choice today to take the road that leads to giving and sowing well into someone's life, and God is sure to send someone in your life that will give to you, too.

39

PRESS FORWARD

~

When you go through life, you will face stumbling blocks, detours, and stop signs, but I encourage you to press forward. You are a winner, a conqueror, a child of God. He has you.

Whatever it is that you would like to do or be, remember you can do and be it. If someone tells you that something is not for you, you must always remember that you will never know until you try. Do not let what anyone says or thinks of you stop you from moving forward and obtaining good things as you travel your journey of life.

Always seek God about everything. Ask Him if it is best for you. Ask Him which way to go, and follow His directions. He knows what is best, He cares about you, and He wants you to make the right decisions in your life.

40

TELL GOD

~

Tell God how much you love Him. Tell God how much you adore Him. Tell God how much you honor Him. Tell God how much you thank Him. Tell God how worthy He is. Tell God He is the One you can depend on no matter what situation you encounter in life. Tell God just how special He is in your life.

Tell God about the miracle you need Him to manifest in your life. Tell God about the promotion you desire. Tell God about how your heart has been hurting. Tell God what you desire to become. Tell Him about all of your problems and concerns. Tell Him about the matter that has been getting the best of you. Tell God whatever it is you need for Him to do in your life. Tell God…He is there to listen to everything you have to say to Him.

41

YOUR HARVEST

~

When you plant your seed, make sure you water it. If you do not water it, it will not grow. Whatever you plant or sow, the harvest will be sure to follow, but only if you talk to God first, and keep it watered. You are your biggest inspiration.

I encourage you to write down your plans, dreams, and goals. Attack them one at a time. The things you thought were or would be too hard, just may turn out to be the easiest thing ever. Go for it!

42

YOUR PART IS IMPORTANT

~

When you do your part, God will do His. Often times we pray and ask God for help, but we are not helping ourselves by doing our part. How bad do we want to change? How bad do we want more? Remember, it starts with you.

Reading His Word is one thing, but getting busy with the actions it takes to help you is another. Make sure you do your part. You have the power to move any mountain in your life with a mustard seed of faith. If the mountain gets too wide, climb over it. If the mountain gets too tall, go around it. Whatever the mountain does, you do the opposite. The choice is yours.

43

NO ROOM

~

The Bible tells us that the enemy, our adversary, the devil comes to "steal, kill and destroy." If we allow any room in our lives for him to come in, he will cause so much turmoil. My eyes and ears are wide open. Are yours? I encourage you not to give him any room in your life.

You have to make sure you keep a consistent prayer life. Prayer keeps you in the presence of God, and "Prayer changes things," too, no matter what it may be. Even if it is early in the morning, or late at night, God hears you. I have tried it and it works. You should try it, too. The more you pray, the less room you have for the enemy to come into your world and cause chaos.

44

RECOGNIZING THE TRICKS

~

When God has something for you, the enemy will always try to destroy it. You must learn to recognize his tricks and tell him boldly, "Satan, get out of my way. You are evil. The Lord is my power and shield, so you are powerless against me."

If you are struggling with a situation, or confused about a circumstance, it could very well be one of that ole devil's tricks to prevent you from receiving what God has for you. The devil carries the keys to confusion, and he will use anything or anyone to trick you.

I encourage you to stay connected to God and allow Him to show you when the devil is trying to creep in your life and trick you. Always remember that you need to be vigilant (alert, watchful) at all times.

45

SEEK GOD

~

When I pass through angry seas and trouble won't leave me alone, I seek God. At night when I cannot sleep, I put my Bible under my pillow so that God can calm my raging thoughts. You should try it. It works every time.

At times you may feel like you are all alone on your journey, but know that God is always walking right in front of you, paving the way for you. Trust in Him. We cannot continue to fail God and expect Him to give us a supernatural blessing. If you want God to bless you, be obedient, trustworthy, in control of your mind, body and spirit, and be kind to others.

46

HIS JUDGING MATTERS

~

When people do not know your story, they will talk about you and judge you. When they know your story, they will do the same thing. When your life ends on this Earth, people will still talk about you and try to judge you for what you've done. Do not worry about pleasing man. You only need to please God. His judging matters.

47

YOUR PURPOSE

~

You were created with a purpose, and no matter what that purpose may be, give God the glory. Your purpose will not be the same as the next person, so focus on what God called you to do. Whatever it is that God purposed you to do or be, make sure you give it your all. "Your gifts and purpose will make room for you." Now inhale, exhale, and walk in your purpose.

48

BE BETTER, DO BETTER, LIVE BETTER

~

Each day we are awaken by the breath of God, we should strive to be better, do better and live better. Our today should not be like yesterday. What are you going to do today? Will you be doing something that will positively impact your life and the lives of those around you?

Always remember that "What goes around comes around." When you sow good seeds, you can expect a good harvest. When you sow bad seeds and treat people wrong, you can expect to reap the same thing. What kind of seeds are you sowing? Are you ready to be better, do better and live better?

49

LISTEN TO GOD

~

So many times God speaks to us, but we choose not to listen because we want to do and have things our way. Have you ever thought about why your world could be upside down? It could very well be this way because you are trying to do it without God.

You must always listen to God and allow Him to lead you. If you have a plan or desire to do something, make sure you include God in your plan. Show Him your ideas and allow Him to lay the foundation, and you build from there. You will find that as you listen to His voice and follow His guide, your plan will work in your favor.

50

GOD'S POWER

~

God has the power to heal all wounds. That hurt, pain, confusion, bitterness, or resentment you may be dealing with, give it to God. His power is like none other. "His breath is the breeze of forgiveness. His light leads to eyes washed clear of tears, and His love manifests a heart of hope." There's no power like God's Power.

51

NO ONE BUT GOD

Think about the goodness of God. Think about where He has brought you from. Now give Him praise. No one can do you like Him. No one can cover you like Him. No one can love you like Him. "All things are possible through Christ Jesus." Things are "turning around for you," and will begin to work for you and not against you. Even though you have been knocked down, praise God for picking you back up. He is all you will ever need.

52

STEP BACK, SIT DOWN AND ALLOW GOD

Until you step back and sit down…, you will continue to face the same issues in life. Allow God to fight your battles for you. If He needed your assistance, you would not continue to go through like you do. When you ask God to take care of something for you, then you need to fully relinquish it to God and be ready to step back, sit down and allow Him to fix it for you.

53

HOW ARE YOU WALKING

~

Time after time we wonder why we are not prospering or our blessings are not flowing in the way we want them to. I would like to ask a few questions: Are you walking in the path of righteousness? Is your life lined up with God's will? If you answered no to these questions, then I would like to ask, how are you walking?

If you are ashamed to speak of God, and give Him praise, why do you feel He should bless you and be there for you when you need Him? Don't call on Him or speak of Him only when you are in need. I encourage you to make Him part of your everyday life.

54

VENGEANCE IS THE LORD'S

~

"Vengeance is the Lord's" not yours. With that being said, we should find peace in knowing that everything will be alright. God knows exactly how to handle every situation. People will test you, and some will take your kindness for weakness. Some will even try to dig a ditch and set traps for you.

I encourage you to pray hard, and ask God to continue to hold your hand. He will make all your enemies your footstools. Those same ones that hurt you will end up needing you.

55

GET READY

~

Everybody cannot go to your next level with you. Several people and things will drop off at a certain time in your life. Where God is taking you, those people or things do not belong. In the next level of your life, there is no room for negativity, so get ready for all the blessings that God has in store for you.

Some things may not be comfortable, and may not feel good in your life right now, but know that God has His hands on you. Do not succumb to your situation. Get ready! Hold on! You will win.

56

REJOICE AND SAY AMEN

~

God has brought you this far for a reason. He knew when you were knocked down, you would get back up. He knew when that door was shut in your face, another one would open. He knew when that job said no, there was a better one in store for you. No matter what goes on in your life, God has the final say. Whatever your issue may be on today, I challenge you to "Rejoice And Say Amen" because God has everything under control.

PSALM 23

The LORD is my shepherd; I shall not want.

He maketh me to lie down in green pastures: He leadeth me beside the still waters.

He restoreth my soul: he leadeth me in the paths of righteousness for his name's sake.

Yea, though I walk through the valley of the shadow of death, I will fear no evil: for thou art with me; thy rod and thy staff they comfort me.

Thou preparest a table before me in the presence of mine enemies: thou anointest my head with oil; my cup runneth over.

Surely goodness and mercy shall follow me all the days of my life: and I will dwell in the house of the LORD forever.

~NOTES~